SAVE
EARTH'S
ANIMALS!

Endangered Animals
of NORTH AMERICA

Marie Allgor

PowerKiDS
press.

New York

Published in 2011 by The Rosen Publishing Group, Inc.
29 East 21st Street, New York, NY 10010

First Edition

Editor: Jennifer Way
Book Design: Julio Gil

Photo Credits: Cover Karl Weatherly/Getty Images; pp. 4, 5 (top) Jupiterimages/Photos.com/Thinkstock; pp. 5 (inset), 8, 15 (inset),17 (inset), 18 iStockphoto/Thinkstock; pp. 6, 10, 12, 13, 14, 20 Shutterstock.com; p. 7 Pete Ryan/Getty Images; pp. 9, 15 (top) Hemera/Thinkstock; p. 16–17 © J & C Sohns/age fotostock; p. 19 Hope Ryden/Getty Images; p. 21 © James Gerholdt/Peter Arnold, Inc.; p. 22 AbleStock.com/Thinkstock.

Library of Congress Cataloging-in-Publication Data

Allgor, Marie.
  Endangered animals of North America / by Marie Allgor. — 1st ed.
      p. cm. — (Save Earth's animals!)
  Includes index.
  ISBN 978-1-4488-2532-5 (library binding) — ISBN 978-1-4488-2648-3 (pbk.) — ISBN 978-1-4488-2649-0 (6-pack)
  1. Endangered species—North America—Juvenile literature. 2. Wildlife conservation—North America—Juvenile literature. I. Title.
  QL84.A45 2011
  591.68097—dc22
                                          2010023414

Manufactured in the United States of America

CPSIA Compliance Information: Batch #WW11PK: For Further Information contact Rosen Publishing, New York, New York at 1-800-237-9932

Contents

Welcome to North America!

North America reaches from Canada to the hot, wet rain forests of Central America. The United States sits in the middle. North America is home to more than 365 million people. It is also home to thousands of animal **species**. Some of these animals, such as mosquitoes, are plentiful. Other North American animals are in trouble.

Elk are plentiful in North America. They live in the western parts of the United States and Canada.

4

The growth of highways across North America has taken over lands where many of the continent's animals once lived.

In the 1800s, the American bison was hunted almost to extinction. Today their numbers are growing, and people keep track of the health of American bison herds.

Some of North America's animals are endangered. This means they are in danger of dying out. These animals are important to North America's many **ecosystems**, though. Scientists and others are trying to save these endangered animals.

North America's Climate

North America is the third-largest continent on Earth. It has many different **climate zones**. Northern Canada is in the cold and dry Arctic climate zone. In the far south of the continent, there is a tropical climate. It is hot and wet for much of the year.

Temperate rain forests, like the one shown here, are found in the northwestern United States and in southwestern Canada.

This coyote lives in Death Valley National Park, in California. Death Valley has one of the hottest and driest climates in North America.

Most of Canada and the United States is in temperate climate zones. These places have warm summers and cool winters. The southwestern United States is hot and dry year-round. Some places, such as Death Valley, get fewer than 2 inches (5 cm) of rain each year!

Habitats in North America

North America is home to a wide range of **habitats**. There is tundra in the north, in Canada and Alaska. Caribou, seals, and polar bears live there. There are mountain habitats with bighorn sheep and pikas. Elk, bison, and prairie dogs live on grassy plains habitats. Birds, snakes, monkeys, and bugs live in the rain forest habitats in the northwest of the United States and in Central America.

Bighorn sheep live in mountain habitats.

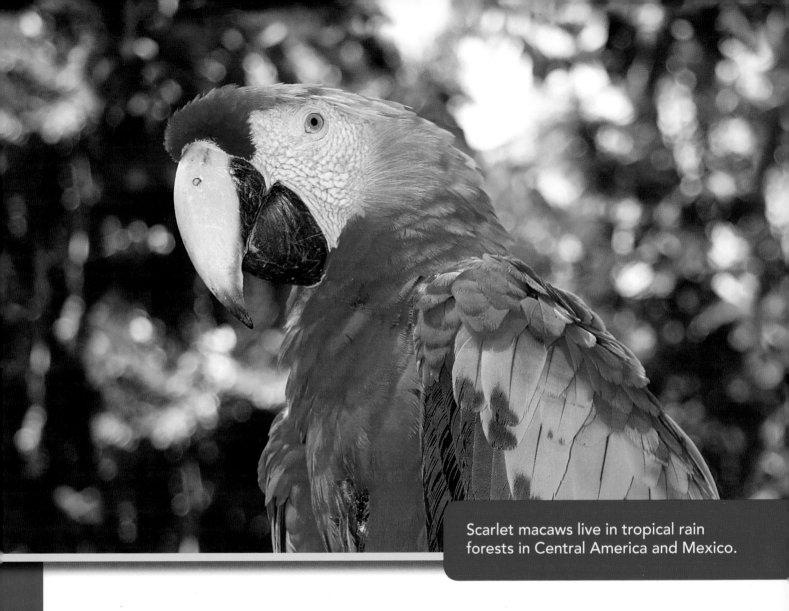

Scarlet macaws live in tropical rain forests in Central America and Mexico.

People have hurt North America's habitats. They destroy them to make room for homes, towns, roads, and farms. People also pollute, or dirty, the places where they live. This pollution hurts many habitats.

North America's Endangered Animals

There are more than 600 species of endangered or **threatened** animals in North America. The animals on these pages are endangered and could one day become **extinct**.

MAP KEY

- California Condor
- Sea Otter
- Pacific Salmon
- American Crocodile
- Utah Prairie Dog
- California Tiger Salamander

California Condor

1. American Crocodile

American crocodiles are **vulnerable** in most of their range. The American crocodile was endangered in Florida. Because of **conservation** work, its numbers there have gone up.

2. California Condor

The California condor became extinct in the wild in 1987. The last six wild birds were caught for a **captive breeding** program that has helped save the condors.

3. Sea Otter

Sea otters live in the oceans off the west coast of Canada, the United States, and Mexico. There were once as many as 300,000 sea otters. Today there are only around 100,000 left.

4. Utah Prairie Dog

Prairie dogs are found only in North America. There are five species, and the Utah prairie dog is one of the two species that are endangered.

5. Pacific Salmon

Pollution, habitat destruction, and overfishing have affected many of North America's fish species. Some species of Pacific salmon are listed as vulnerable, endangered, and **critically** endangered.

6. California Tiger Salamander

The California tiger salamander lives in grasslands and open woodlands in burrows left behind by other animals. These salamanders have lost more than half their habitat in California.

GREENLAND

CANADA

North America

UNITED STATES

MEXICO

THE BAHAMAS

HAITI

CUBA

PUERTO RICO

DOMINICAN REP.

JAMAICA

BELIZE

HONDURAS

GUATEMALA

NICARAGUA

EL SALVADOR

COSTA RICA

PANAMA

California Condors

The California condor is a huge bird. Its wings measure 7 feet (2 m) from tip to tip! It once lived on North America's west coast from Canada to Mexico. Sadly this bird has disappeared from many of the places it once lived.

The California condor nests on cliffs or rocky outcroppings or in high trees in grassy woodlands.

You can see tags on the wings of this California condor. The tags help scientists keep track of the birds' numbers.

So few birds remained in the 1980s that the birds were almost extinct in the wild. To help these birds, scientists added the last six wild birds to a captive breeding program. Some condors have now been put back into their natural habitat. Seven chicks have been born in the wild since then. California condors are still critically endangered, however.

Sea Otters

Sea otters are marine animals. This means they spend their lives in the ocean. They live close to the shore, often in places with lots of kelp, or seaweed. Sea otters live mostly in the Pacific Ocean. Sea otters have fur that keeps their bodies warm in the cold ocean waters. They spend a lot of time keeping their fur clean.

Sea otters eat many different sea animals, including sea urchins, octopuses, and shellfish.

Orcas, also known as killer whales, eat sea otters.

Bald eagles, brown bears, and coyotes have also been known to kill sea otters.

Sea otters face many dangers. Killer whales and sharks kill many sea otters each year. Many sea otters die from illnesses, too. Their biggest threats from people are oil spills and getting caught in fishing nets.

Utah Prairie Dogs

Prairie dogs are related to squirrels. They live on the grasslands of the United States and Mexico. Prairie dogs dig tunnels under the ground and live in groups.

Utah prairie dogs are the smallest species of prairie dog.

Prairie dog homes are made up of groups of tunnels that connect to one another. These groups of tunnels are called towns.

Most species of prairie dogs are doing well. Utah prairie dogs are endangered, though. They once lived across the state of Utah. Today they live only in a very small part of the southwestern corner of Utah. For a long time, they were killed as pests. They were also killed by droughts, illnesses, and loss of habitat due to farming and grazing. Work is being done to help the Utah prairie dog.

Red Wolves

Red wolves were once widespread in the United States in the Southeast and on the East Coast. Scientists guess that they once lived in wetland habitats, forests, and coastal prairies.

The red wolf became extinct in the wild in the 1980s. It had been hunted by people, killed by illnesses, and had lost a lot of its natural habitat.

Red wolves hunt raccoons. They also hunt deer and rabbits.

The red wolf is a subspecies of the gray wolf. A subspecies is a small group within a species.

Red wolves that had been bred in captivity have since been reintroduced into the wild. Today, only around 100 red wolves live in the wild in eastern North Carolina. They are still critically endangered, but there is hope for the future of red wolves!

California Tiger Salamanders

California tiger salamanders live in only a small part of California. They breed in **vernal pools** and other bodies of water. However, they have lost more than half of their habitat and around three-quarters of their breeding places! Because of this, their numbers are dropping.

Habitat loss is one of the reasons that the California tiger salamander is in trouble. The places where it once lived now have roads and homes built on them.

California tiger salamanders make their homes in grasslands or in open woodlands, where they take over burrows left by other animals.

California tiger salamanders are now vulnerable to becoming extinct. This means that they are not endangered yet, but they could be in a few years. When an animal is listed as vulnerable, it means there is still time to save this animal. People must work hard to help them, though.

Save North America's Animals!

One of the jobs of the U.S. Fish and Wildlife Service is to let people know which animals are in trouble. This group comes up with **recovery** plans, sets aside conservation lands, and teaches people.

The conservation program for the gray wolf is one example of a successful program. People had hunted this animal because they feared it, and it sometimes killed farm animals and pets. Its habitat was getting smaller and there were fewer of the animals it hunted for food. However, conservation programs helped save the gray wolf from becoming extinct.

Glossary

CAPTIVE BREEDING (KAP-tiv BREED-ing) Bringing animals together to have babies in a zoo or an aquarium instead of in the wild.

CLIMATE ZONES (KLY-mut ZOHNZ) Large places that have the same kind of weather.

CONSERVATION (kon-sur-VAY-shun) Keeping something from being hurt.

CRITICALLY (KRIH-tih-kuh-lee) Being at a turning point.

ECOSYSTEMS (EE-koh-sis-temz) Communities of living things and the kinds of land in which they live.

EXTINCT (ik-STINGKT) No longer existing.

HABITATS (HA-beh-tats) The kinds of land where animals or plants naturally live.

RECOVERY (rih-KUH-ver-ee) Getting something back.

SPECIES (SPEE-sheez) One kind of living thing. All people are one species.

THREATENED (THREH-tund) Could be hurt.

VERNAL POOLS (VER-nul POOLZ) Small ponds that have water only part of the year, have no streams flowing in, and have no fish.

VULNERABLE (VUL-neh-reh-bul) Open to being hurt.

Index

Web Sites

Due to the changing nature of Internet links, PowerKids Press has developed an online list of Web sites related to the subject of this book. This site is updated regularly. Please use this link to access the list: www.powerkidslinks.com/sea/noamer/